ENGLI...
Picture Dictionary

Catherine Bruzzone and Louise Millar

Illustrations by Louise Comfort and Steph Dix

b small publishing

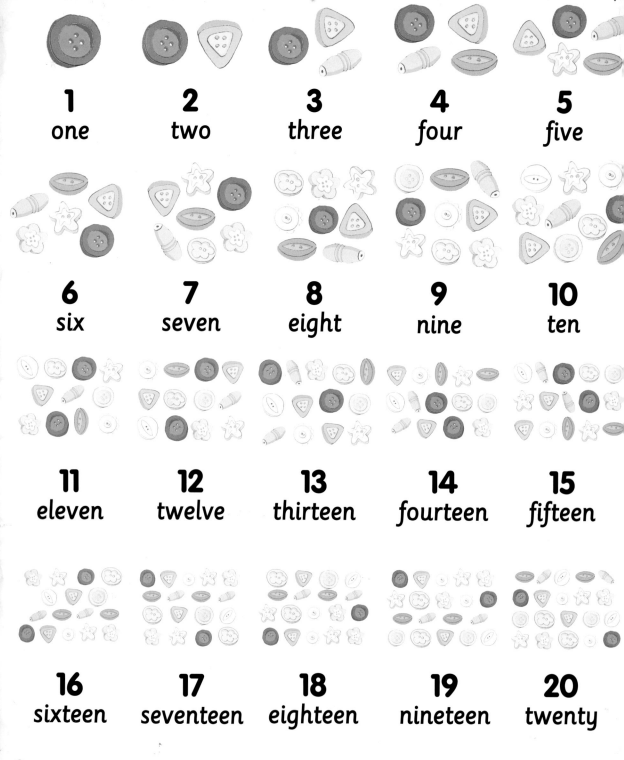

1
one

2
two

3
three

4
four

5
five

6
six

7
seven

8
eight

9
nine

10
ten

11
eleven

12
twelve

13
thirteen

14
fourteen

15
fifteen

16
sixteen

17
seventeen

18
eighteen

19
nineteen

20
twenty

Contents

Numbers 1-20	2	Baby animals	23
The body	4	At the beach	24
Clothes	5	Under the sea	25
The family	6	The zoo	26
The house	7	Toys	27
In the house	8	Party time!	28
The kitchen	9	The classroom	29
The bedroom	10	Sports	30
The bathroom	11	Weather	31
The town	12	Action words	32
The street	13	Storybook words	33
Vehicles	14	The building site	34
The park	15	Tools	35
The hospital	16	Luggage	36
The supermarket	17	Rail travel	37
Fruit	18	Air travel	38
Vegetables	19	At sea	39
The country	20	Opposites	40
In the forest	21	Word list	42
The farm	22	Colours	48

childcare

The body

head

eyes

nose

mouth

shoulders

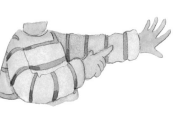

arm

hand

leg

foot

Clothes

skirt

dress

trousers

coat

shirt

pyjamas

shoes

socks

hat

The family

mother/
Mummy

father/
Daddy

sister

brother

grandmother

grandfather

aunt

uncle

cousins

The house

kitchen

sitting room

bedroom

bathroom

toilet

stairs

floor

ceiling

garden

In the house

sofa

armchair

cushion

curtains

picture

stool

telephone

computer

television

The kitchen

sink

fridge

cooker

knife

spoon

fork

plate

glass

saucepan

The bedroom

bed

chest of drawers

wardrobe

alarm clock

hairbrush

shelf

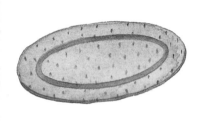

rug

window

door

The bathroom

washbasin

toilet

bath

shower

mirror

towel

toothpaste

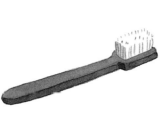
toothbrush

soap

The town

house

school

station

shop

post office

supermarket

factory

market

cinema

The street

street

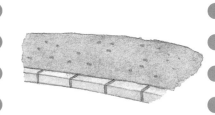

pavement

bus stop

traffic lights

roundabout

streetlamp

road sign

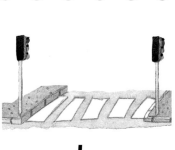

zebra crossing

police

Vehicles

bus

ambulance

bicycle

car

police car

motorbike

lorry

fire engine

van

The park

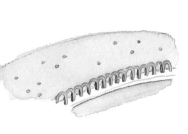

path

see-saw

swing

girl

boy

child

lake

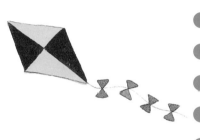

kite

bench

15

The hospital

doctor

nurse

x-ray

thermometer

medicine

bandage

plaster

crutches

wheelchair

The supermarket

egg

bread

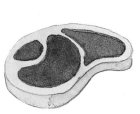

meat

rice

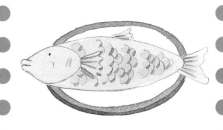

fish

butter

milk

pasta

sugar

Fruit

apple

peach

cherry

orange

pineapple

mango

banana

grapes

strawberry

Vegetables

potato

corn

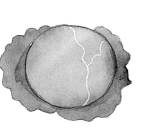

cabbage

courgette

carrot

aubergine

tomato

lettuce

celery

The country

tree

grass

flower

field

forest

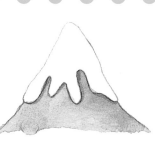

mountain

bridge

river

bird

In the forest

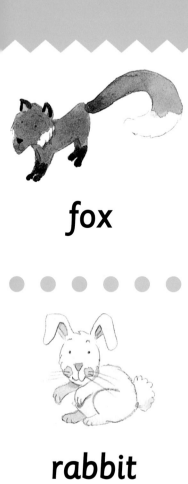

fox

squirrel

deer

rabbit

brown bear

butterfly

beetle

caterpillar

fly

The farm

cat

mouse

dog

cow

horse

pig

sheep

duck

goat

Baby animals

puppy

kitten

foal

calf

chick

cygnet

duckling

lamb

piglet

At the beach

sea

seagull

sand

fish

seaweed

shell

rock

sailing boat

wave

Under the sea

octopus

starfish

jellyfish

lobster

shark

whale

wreck

diver

coral

The zoo

giraffe

snake

hippopotamus

dolphin

tiger

crocodile

polar bear

lion

elephant

Toys

teddy

robot

ball

puzzle

toy train

game

doll

paints

drum

Party time!

sandwich

chocolate

chips

pizza

cake

ice-cream

coke

orange juice

water

The classroom

teacher

table

chair

book

coloured
pencil

glue

paper

pen

scissors

Sports

football

table tennis

skiing

gymnastics

cycling

athletics

fishing

swimming

basketball

Weather

sun

hot

rain

cloud

wind

storm

fog

cold

snow

Action words

running

walking

crawling

carrying

standing

sitting

pushing

hugging

pulling

Storybook words

dragon

mermaid

knight

pirate

fairy

witch

prince

princess

castle

The building site

digger

cement mixer

crane

scaffolding

dumper truck

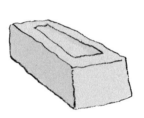

brick

bulldozer

ladder

wood

Tools

rake

spade

bucket

wheelbarrow

hammer

nail

saw

hose

paintbrush

Luggage

suitcase

satchel

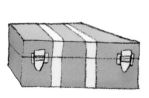

trunk

rucksack

handbag

briefcase

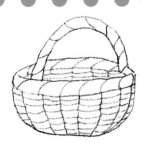

basket

shopping bag

purse

Air travel

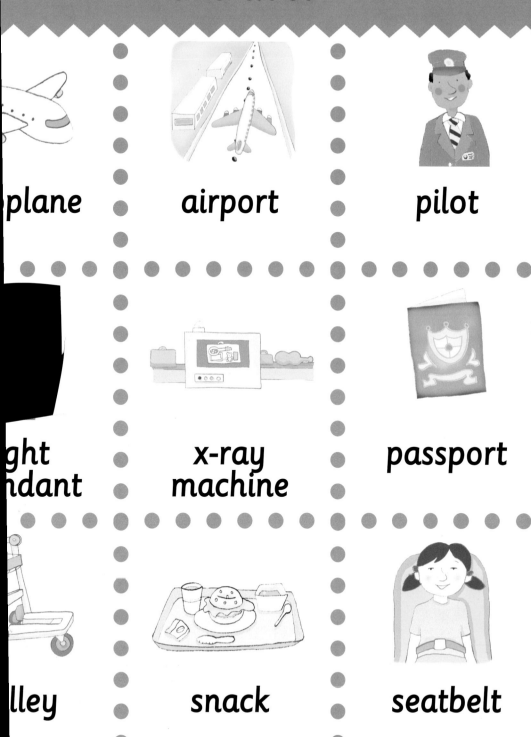

plane

airport

pilot

ght
ndant

x-ray
machine

passport

lley

snack

seatbelt

Rail travel

ticket

ticket
collector

platf

train driver

signal

tra

seat

level crossing

ra

At sea

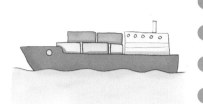

ship

yacht

rowing boat

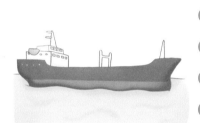

tanker

fishing boat

ferry

buoy

port

lighthouse

Opposites

friendly

angry

thin

clean

dirty

tidy

sad

happy

heavy

Opposites

fat

tall

short

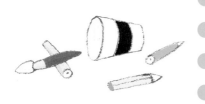

messy

fast

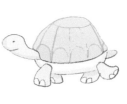

slow

light

beautiful

ugly

Word list

	page
aeroplane	38
airport	38
alarm clock	10
ambulance	14
angry	40
apple	18
arm	4
armchair	8
athletics	30
aubergine	19
aunt	6
ball	27
banana	18
bandage	16
basket	36
basketball	30
bath	11
bathroom	7
beach	24
beautiful	41
bed	10
bedroom	7
beetle	21
bench	15
bicycle	14
bird	20
black	48
blue	48
body	4
book	29

boy	15
bread	17
brick	34
bridge	20
briefcase	36
brother	6
brown	48
brown bear	21
bucket	35
building site	34
bulldozer	34
buoy	39
bus	14
bus stop	13
butter	17
butterfly	21
cabbage	19
cake	28
calf	23
car	14
carrot	19
carrying	32
castle	33
cat	22
caterpillar	21
ceiling	7
celery	19
cement mixer	34
chair	29
cherry	18
chest of drawers	10

chick	23	dirty	40
child	15	diver	25
chips	28	doctor	16
chocolate	28	dog	22
cinema	12	doll	27
classroom	29	dolphin	26
clean	40	door	10
clothes	5	dragon	33
cloud	31	dress	5
coat	5	drum	27
cola	28	duck	22
cold	31	duckling	23
coloured pencil	29	dumper truck	34
colours	48	egg	17
computer	8	eight	2
cooker	9	eighteen	2
coral	25	elephant	26
corn	19	eleven	2
country	20	eyes	4
courgette	19	factory	12
cousins	6	fairy	33
cow	22	family	7
crane	34	farm	22
crawling	32	fast	41
crocodile	26	fat	41
crutches	16	father	6
curtains	8	ferry	39
cushion	8	field	20
cycling	30	fifteen	2
cygnet	23	fire engine	14
Daddy	6	fish	17, 24
deer	21	fishing	30
digger	34	fishing boat	39

five	2	happy	40
flight attendant	38	hat	5
floor	7	head	4
flower	20	heavy	40
fly	21	hippopotamus	26
foal	23	horse	22
fog	31	hose	35
foot	4	hospital	16
football	30	hot	31
forest	20	house	7
fork	9	hugging	32
four	2	ice-cream	28
fourteen	2	jellyfish	25
fox	21	kitchen	7, 9
fridge	9	kite	15
friendly	40	kitten	23
fruit	18	knife	9
garden	7	knight	33
giraffe	26	ladder	34
girl	15	lake	15
glass	9	lamb	23
glue	29	leg	4
goat	22	lettuce	19
grandfather	6	level crossing	37
grandmother	6	light	41
grapes	18	lighthouse	39
grass	20	lion	26
green	48	lobster	25
gymnastics	30	lorry	14
hairbrush	10	luggage	36
hammer	35	mango	18
hand	4	market	12
handbag	36	meat	17

medicine	16	piglet	23
mermaid	33	pilot	38
messy	41	pineapple	18
milk	17	pirate	33
mirror	11	pizza	28
mother	6	plaster	16
motorbike	14	plate	9
mountain	20	platform	37
mouse	22	polar bear	26
mouth	4	police	13
Mummy	6	police car	14
nail	35	port	39
nine	2	post office	12
nineteen	2	potato	19
nose	4	prince	33
nurse	16	princess	33
octopus	25	pulling	32
one	2	puppy	23
orange (fruit)	18	purple	48
orange (colour)	48	purse	36
orange juice	28	pushing	32
paintbrush	35	puzzle	27
paints	27	pyjamas	5
paper	29	rabbit	21
party	28	rails	37
passport	38	rain	31
pasta	17	rake	35
path	15	red	48
pavement	13	rice	17
peach	18	river	20
pen	29	road sign	13
picture	8	robot	27
pig	22	rock	24

roundabout	13	shoulders	4
rowing boat	39	shower	11
rucksack	36	signal	37
rug	10	sink	9
running	32	sister	6
sad	40	sitting	32
sailing boat	24	sitting room	7
sand	24	six	2
sandwich	28	sixteen	2
satchel	36	skiing	30
saucepan	9	skirt	5
saw	35	slow	41
scaffolding	34	snack	38
school	12	snake	26
scissors	29	snow	31
sea	24	soap	11
seagull	24	socks	5
seat	37	sofa	8
seatbelt	38	spade	35
seaweed	24	spoon	9
see-saw	15	sports	30
seven	2	squirrel	21
seventeen	2	stairs	7
shark	25	standing	32
sheep	22	starfish	25
shelf	10	station	12
shell	24	stool	8
ship	39	storm	31
shirt	5	strawberry	18
shoes	5	street	13
shop	12	streetlamp	13
shopping bag	36	sugar	17
short	41	suitcase	36

sun	31	tree	20
supermarket	12	trolley	38
swimming	30	trousers	5
table	29	trunk	36
table tennis	30	twelve	2
tall	41	twenty	2
tanker	39	two	2
teacher	29	ugly	41
teddy	27	uncle	6
telephone	8	van	14
television	8	vegetables	19
ten	2	vehicles	14
thermometer	16	walking	32
thin	40	wardrobe	10
thirteen	2	washbasin	11
three	2	water	28
ticket	37	wave	24
ticket collector	37	weather	31
tidy	40	whale	25
tiger	26	wheelbarrow	35
toilet	7	wheelchair	16
tomato	19	white	48
tools	35	wind	31
toothbrush	11	window	10
toothpaste	11	witch	33
towel	11	wood	34
town	12	wreck	25
toy	27	x-ray	16
toy train	27	x-ray machine	38
traffic lights	13	yacht	39
train	37	yellow	48
train driver	37	zebra crossing	13
travel	37	zoo	26

Colours

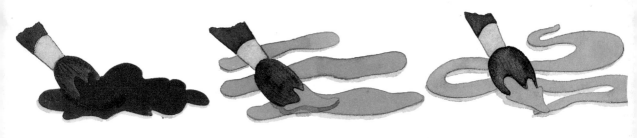

red   blue   green

yellow   black   orange

white   purple   brown